# Instant Android Fragmentation Management How-to

A complete hands-on guide to solving the biggest problem facing Android application developers today

**Gianluca Pacchiella**

PUBLISHING

BIRMINGHAM - MUMBAI

# Instant Android Fragmentation Management How-to

First published: January 2013

Production Reference: 1160113

Published by Packt Publishing Ltd.
Livery Place
35 Livery Street
Birmingham B3 2PB, UK.

ISBN 978-1-78216-086-1

www.packtpub.com

# Credits

**Author**

Gianluca Pacchiella

**Reviewers**

Rick Boyer

Visar Shehu

**Acquisition Editor**

Martin Bell

**Commissioning Editor**

Maria D'souza

**Technical Editor**

Prasad Dalvi

**Copy Editor**

Aditya Nair

**Project Coordinator**

Priya Sharma

**Proofreader**

Maria Gould

**Production Coordinator**

Prachali Bhiwandkar

**Cover Work**

Prachali Bhiwandkar

**Cover Image**

Sheetal Aute

# About the Author

**Gianluca Pacchiella** is an Italian developer living in Turin. He has a Master's degree in Physics and a PhD in Mathematics. He started programming in 2000 with some weird web languages (PHP, MySQL, HTML4, and CSS), but soon he was fascinated by real programming on the UNIX systems, and fell in love with C language (and a little bit of assembly).

Some years later, Gianluca bought an Android phone and started to learn everything about it and about embedded systems. Meanwhile, he continued to improve his skills with the web application, using the Python language and the Django framework together with the Nginx web server and the PostgreSQL database.

In his spare time, he tries to learn security concepts and cryptography applied to his projects.

# About the Reviewers

**Rick Boyer** is an Android developer with over 20 years of programming experience, with a passion for mobile development. Having programmed on different mobile devices, including Windows CE, Windows Phone, and Android, he now focuses solely on Android with his consulting business, NightSky Development. He also runs a LinkedIn forum focusing on developers bringing their apps to the market.

He can be contacted via www.linkedin.com/in/boyerrick, www.NightSkyDev.com, and LinkenIn Android Group at goo.gl/Byilc.

**Visar Shehu** has a PhD in Computer Science and is currently employed at the Computer Science department of South East European University in Tetovo, Macedonia. His research interests focus on intelligent web and mobile technologies that aim to integrate statistical and data mining techniques in building adaptable user interfaces and applications. Visar Shehu has been involved in multiple research projects and has authored and co-authored a number of research papers. Besides his academic work, he has also contributed in the development of various information systems ranging from mobile applications, custom-built content management, and learning management systems.

# www.PacktPub.com

## Support files, eBooks, discount offers and more

You might want to visit www.PacktPub.com for support files and downloads related to your book.

Did you know that Packt offers eBook versions of every book published, with PDF and ePub files available? You can upgrade to the eBook version at www.PacktPub.com and as a print book customer, you are entitled to a discount on the eBook copy. Get in touch with us at service@packtpub.com for more details.

At www.PacktPub.com, you can also read a collection of free technical articles, sign up for a range of free newsletters and receive exclusive discounts and offers on Packt books and eBooks.

http://PacktLib.PacktPub.com

Do you need instant solutions to your IT questions? PacktLib is Packt's online digital book library. Here, you can access, read and search across Packt's entire library of books.

## Why Subscribe?

- ► Fully searchable across every book published by Packt
- ► Copy and paste, print and bookmark content
- ► On demand and accessible via web browser

## Free Access for Packt account holders

If you have an account with Packt at www.PacktPub.com, you can use this to access PacktLib today and view nine entirely free books. Simply use your login credentials for immediate access.

# Table of Contents

# Preface

Smartphones, by now, have entered our lives not only as users and consumers but also as producers of our own content. Though this kind of device has been on the market since 1992 (the first was the Simon model by IBM), the big diffusion was driven by Apple's iPhone, when it was produced in 2007 (this year, the fifth generation of this device has been released).

Meanwhile, another big giant, Google, developed an open source product to be used as the internal operating system in mobile devices; in a different manner from the leader of the market, this company doesn't constraint itself to a unique hardware-specific device, but allows third-party companies to use it on their cell phones, which have different characteristics. The big advantage was also to be able to sell this device to consumers that don't want to (or can't have) spend as much money as the Apple phone costs. This allowed Android to win the battle of diffusion.

But there is another side to the coin. A variety of devices by different producers means more fragmentation of the underlying system and a non-uniform user experience that can be really disappointing. As programmers, we have to take into account these problems and this book strives to be a useful guideline to solve that problem.

## What this book covers

*Installing the compatibility package (Must know)*, provides Google's primary solution to the backward compatibility problem.

*Fragments (Should know)*, discusses the first new feature introduced with the new Android release. This recipe also explains how to create the context-adapting UI.

*Loader (Should know)*, discusses how the smoothness of an Android application is guaranteed using the built-in utilities that allow us to do expensive work in the background.

*ActionBar (Should know)*, discusses the standard way to create an appealing UI that manages user interactions with our applications.

# What you need for this book

In order to follow the steps in this book, you only need to know the Android platform and be able to compile and install applications. Some examples include the use of the Eclipse IDE, but it is not mandatory for understanding the steps.

# Who this book is for

The target audience of this book are the programmers that already know how to program the Android platform, and want to know how to write well-behaving applications that are backward compatible with almost the entire Android ecosystems.

# Conventions

In this book, you will find a number of styles of text that distinguish between different kinds of information. Here are some examples of these styles, and an explanation of their meaning.

Code words in text are shown as follows: "The JAR file to add to the project is `<AndroidSDK>\extras\android\support\v4\android-support-v4.jar`."

A block of code is set as follows:

```
public class FragmentCompatibility extends FragmentActivity {
    ...
}
```

**New terms** and **important words** are shown in bold. Words that you see on the screen, in menus or dialog boxes for example, appear in the text like this: "Launch the Android SDK Manager from Eclipse, selecting **Window | Android SDK Manager**."

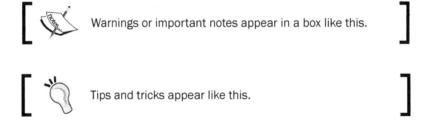

Warnings or important notes appear in a box like this.

Tips and tricks appear like this.

# Reader feedback

Feedback from our readers is always welcome. Let us know what you think about this book—what you liked or may have disliked. Reader feedback is important for us to develop titles that you really get the most out of.

To send us general feedback, simply send an e-mail to feedback@packtpub.com, and mention the book title via the subject of your message.

If there is a book that you need and would like to see us publish, please send us a note in the **SUGGEST A TITLE** form on www.packtpub.com or e-mail suggest@packtpub.com.

If there is a topic that you have expertise in and you are interested in either writing or contributing to a book, see our author guide on www.packtpub.com/authors.

# Customer support

Now that you are the proud owner of a Packt book, we have a number of things to help you to get the most from your purchase.

## Downloading the example code

You can download the example code files for all Packt books you have purchased from your account at http://www.PacktPub.com. If you purchased this book elsewhere, you can visit http://www.PacktPub.com/support and register to have the files e-mailed directly to you.

## Errata

Although we have taken every care to ensure the accuracy of our content, mistakes do happen. If you find a mistake in one of our books—maybe a mistake in the text or the code—we would be grateful if you would report this to us. By doing so, you can save other readers from frustration and help us improve subsequent versions of this book. If you find any errata, please report them by visiting http://www.packtpub.com/support, selecting your book, clicking on the **errata submission form** link, and entering the details of your errata. Once your errata are verified, your submission will be accepted and the errata will be uploaded on our website, or added to any list of existing errata, under the Errata section of that title. Any existing errata can be viewed by selecting your title from http://www.packtpub.com/support.

# Piracy

Piracy of copyright material on the Internet is an ongoing problem across all media. At Packt, we take the protection of our copyright and licenses very seriously. If you come across any illegal copies of our works, in any form, on the Internet, please provide us with the location address or website name immediately so that we can pursue a remedy.

Please contact us at copyright@packtpub.com with a link to the suspected pirated material.

We appreciate your help in protecting our authors, and our ability to bring you valuable content.

# Questions

You can contact us at questions@packtpub.com if you are having a problem with any aspect of the book, and we will do our best to address it.

# Instant Android Fragmentation Management How-to

Welcome to *Instant Android Fragmentation Management How-to*.

One of the biggest challenges Android developers face is the fragmentation of the operating system. If we look at the following distribution graph, we can see that there are three major versions of the Android OS—Froyo, Gingerbread, and Ice Cream Sandwich (ICS)—each with its own look, behavior, and API libraries:

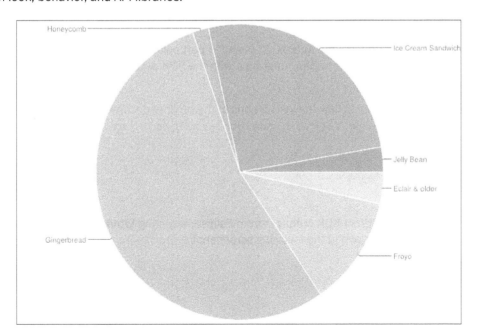

Because of these differences between the releases, the effort required in writing applications that work seamlessly on all the devices out there can be exhausting. This How-to should reduce the stress, providing you with some ready-to-use techniques to address these problems.

**Downloading the example code**

You can download the example code files for all Packt books you have purchased from your account at http://www.PacktPub.com. If you purchased this book elsewhere, you can visit http://www.PacktPub. com/support and register to have the files e-mailed directly to you.

# Installing the compatibility package (Must know)

As the name implies, Support Library provides support for the latest APIs on older versions of the Android OS. This brings many of the latest features, such as Fragments, to the earlier OS releases.

Additional information can be found in the appropriate section on the official Android Developer site at http://developer.android.com/tools/extras/support-library.html.

## Getting ready

Before following the next sections you need to install all the tools that allow you to write, compile, and install programs into your Android device or emulator.

The standard way is to install the Android SDK and in particular the Android Developer Tool, a plugin for the Eclipse IDE. It provides integration with the SDK and a bunch of utilities to help with your development.

In order to install this tool, follow the instructions in the original documentation that you can find at http://developer.android.com/tools/help/adt.html.

## How to do it...

Let's install the library:

1. Launch the Android SDK Manager from Eclipse, selecting **Window | Android SDK Manager**, as shown in the following screenshot:

2. You will be presented with the list of all available packages (installed or not). Scroll down until you reach the **Extras** section and select **Android Support Library**; now you can click on the **install packages** button in the lower-right corner and wait several minutes (the time depends on the quality of your Internet connection):

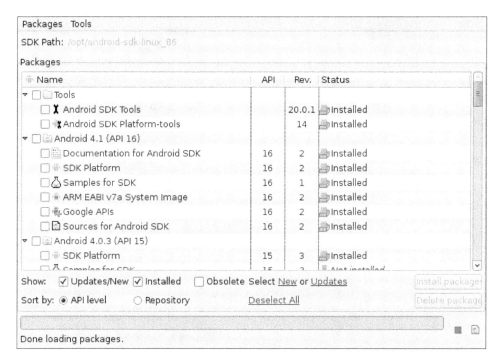

The support library files will be downloaded to the Android SDK folder. The JAR file to add to the project is `<AndroidSDK>\extras\android\support\v4\android-support-v4.jar`.

Let us reference this library from your Android project:

1. Copy the Support Library into the `libs` directory at the root of your project (create it if doesn't exist).

2. Open your project in Eclipse and select the element corresponding to the Support Library from **Package explorer**. Right-click and select **Build Path** | **Add to build path** from the menu.

3. The final step is to check if the setup is working correctly. To do this, add the following import to a project and verify that there are no errors in Eclipse:

   ```
   import android.support.v4.app.FragmentActivity;
   ```

4. Build the project:

If there are no build errors, everything is ok.

## How it works...

An Android application is first of all a Java application, and like all these kinds of applications, it needs to know where to look for the classes used in your code; this is simply done by adding the library of your choice to the build path. Normally in Java, the libraries' path is indicated by the JAVAPATH environmental variable, but since Eclipse uses its system, the details are more subtle but the concepts are the same.

## There's more...

Now let's talk about some other options, or possibly some pieces of general information that are relevant to this task.

### API levels

To better understand about the compatibility package, it's helpful to know a bit about Android's history.

The Android platform was born in 2003, as the product of a company which at first was known as Android Inc. and which was acquired by Google in 2005. Its direct competitors were and are still today the iOS platform by Apple and the RIM, know as Blackberry. Technically speaking, its core is an operating system using a Linux Kernel, aimed to be installed on devices with very different hardware (mainly mobile devices, but today it is also used in general embedded systems like, for example, the game console OUYA that features a modified version of Android 4.0).

Like any software that has been around for a while, many changes happened to the functionality and many versions came out, each with a name of a dessert:

- ▸ Apple Pie (API level 1)
- ▸ Banana Bread (API level 2)
- ▸ 1.5 – Cupcake (API level 3)
- ▸ 1.6 – Donut (API level 4)
- ▸ 2.0-2.1x – Eclair (API level 5 to 7)
- ▸ 2.2 – Froyo (API level 8)
- ▸ 2.3 – Gingerbread (API level 9 and 10)
- ▸ 3.0-3.2 – Honeycomb (API level 11 to 13)
- ▸ 4.0 – Ice Cream Sandwich (API level 14 and 15)
- ▸ 4.1 – Jelly Bean (API level 16)

Like in many other software projects, the names, as well as the themes, are in alphabetical order (another project that follows this approach is the Ubuntu distribution).

The **API level** written in the parenthesis is the main point about this compatibility package. Each version of software introduces or removes features and bugs. In its lifetime, an operating system such as Android aims to add more fantastic innovations while avoiding breaking pre-installed applications in older versions, but also aims to make available to these older versions the same features with a process technically called **backporting**.

For more information about the API levels, carefully read the official documentation available at `http://developer.android.com/guide/topics/manifest/uses-sdk-element.html#ApiLevels`.

All that you will read in the following sections is thought to address these problems, using backporting; in particular, to specifically address the backward compatibility issues with version 3.0 of the Android operating system—the version named Honeycomb.

Version 3.0 was first intended to be installed on tablets, and in general, on devices with large screens. Android is a platform that from the beginning was intended to be used on devices with very different characteristics (think a system where an application must be usable on VGA screens, with or without physical keyboards, with a camera, and so on); with the release of 3.0, all this was improved with specific APIs thought to extend and make developing applications easier, and also to create new patterns with the graphical user interface.

The more important innovation was the introduction of the Fragment class. Earlier, the only main class in developing the Android applications was Activity, a class that provides the user with a screen in order to accomplish a specific task, but that was too coarse grain and not re-usable enough to be used in the applications with large screens such as a tablet. With the introduction of the Fragment class to be used as the basic block, it is now possible to create responsive mobile design; that is, producing content adapting to the context and optimizing the block's placement, using reflowing or a combination of each Fragment inside the main Activity.

These are concepts inspired by the so called responsive web design, where developers build web pages that adapt to the viewport's size; the preeminent book about this argument is *Responsive Web Design, Ethan Marcotte*.

If all this seems a bit complicated, allow me to make a simple example using a real application. The following image is the composition of two screenshots of the same application (Google Play, the Android Market) with two different screen resolutions; you can see how the information about the developer and the information about the application is placed side by side on the tablet version, where as in the phone version they are just shown one below the other.

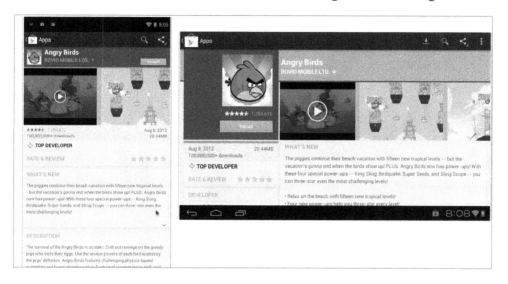

It's not the only possibility to create a so-called multi-paned layout; you can stretch, compress, stack, or expand the Fragment depending on your plan. On the Android's site, it's available as a guide worth following—in the design section of the site. It is available at `http://developer.android.com/design/patterns/multi-pane-layouts.html`.

Another important element introduced in Google's platform is the UI pattern named ActionBar—a piece of interface at the top of an application where the more important menu's buttons are visualized in order to be easily accessible.

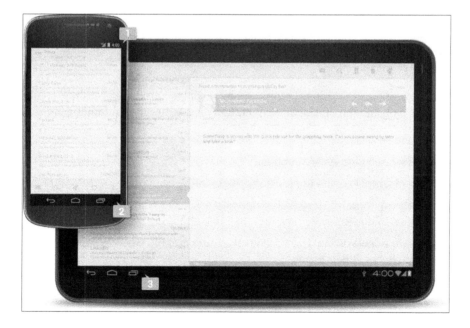

Also a new contextual menu is available in the action bar. When, for example, one or more items in a list are selected (such as, the Gmail application), the appearance of the bar changes and shows new buttons related to the actions available for the selected items.

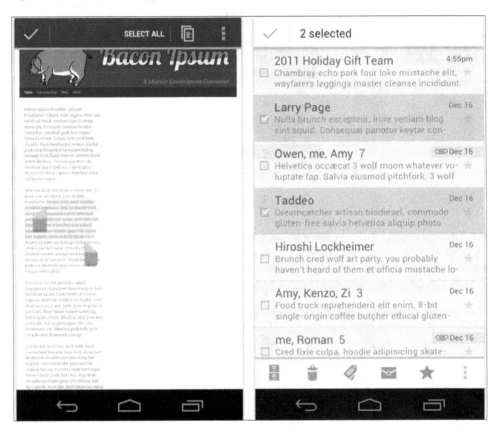

For sake of completeness, let me list other new capabilities introduced with Honeycomb (as previously said, look into the official documentation for a better understanding of them):

- **Copy and Paste**: A clipboard-based framework
- **Loaders**: Load data asynchronously
- **Drag and Drop**: Permits the moving of data between views
- **Property animation framework**: Supersedes the old Animation package, allowing the animation of almost everything into an application
- **Hardware acceleration**: From API level 11, the graphic pipeline uses dedicated hardware when it is present
- Support for encrypted storage

Not all the things listed here are backported with the Support Library. In particular, there is no official way to implement the new animation framework in a backward compatible way (libraries that do this do exist though).

Unfortunately, the Support Library does not support all these features of previous versions of the OS. Most notably, the official Google Support Library does not support the action bar.

Fortunately, for Android developers, there is an open-source project called `ActionBarSherlock`, which does a fantastic job of bringing the ActionBar API back to Android 1.6 (API level 4). We will discuss more on this in the *ActionBar* section.

# Fragments (Should know)

This is the most important section. Here you will learn how to create an Android application designed to be not only backwards compatible with versions down to API level 4, but also capable of showing contents depending on the context. In a phone with normal-size display, it will only show a list (single-paned configuration), but when a larger screen is available, a view with the details of the selection is also displayed (multi-paned configuration).

## How to do it...

Let's start creating a simple application composed of a single Activity and two Fragments. One shows a list of items and the second one shows the data related to the selection.

1.  Import all the necessary classes:

    ```
    import android.content.*;
    import android.support.v4.app.*;
    import android.view.*;
    import android.widget.*;
    import android.os.Bundle;
    ```

2.  Define the Activity that will contain all the code, extending the `FragmentActivity` class from the Support Library:

    ```
    public class FragmentCompatibility extends FragmentActivity {
        ...
    }
    ```

3.  Implement its method `onCreate()`, where we are going to set the initial layout and do what is necessary in order to manage it:

    ```
    @Override
    public void onCreate(Bundle savedInstanceState) {
        super.onCreate(savedInstanceState);
        setContentView(R.layout.main);
    ```

```
/*
 * There is the main_container view so we are not
   in multi paned
 * and we attach the fragment at runtime (we can
   not modify lately
 * the fragment organization if it's defined in
   XML)
 */
boolean isMultiPaned = (findViewBy
Id(R.id.main_container) == null);
if (!isMultiPaned) {

  /*
   * If we are coming from a previous instance we don't
   * have to reattach the SmallListFragment.
   */
  if (savedInstanceState != null) {
    return;
  }
  SmallListFragment slf = new SmallListFragment();

  getSupportFragmentManager().beginTransaction()
  .add(R.id.main_container, slf).commit();
  }
}
```

4.  Create the Fragment showing the list of primary options using `ListFragment`:

```
public static class SmallListFragment extends ListFragment {
      ....
}
```

5.  Implement the `onActivityCreate()` method for this class, where we set the content of the list:

```
@Override
public void onActivityCreated(Bundle b) {
  super.onActivityCreated(b);
  setListAdapter(
    new ArrayAdapter<String>(getActivity(),
    android.R.layout.simple_list_item_1,
    itemTitleArray
    )
  );
  // First, we need to understand if is multi paned
  mIsMultiPaned = (getActivity()
  .findViewById(R.id.main_container) == null);

}
```

6. Implement the `onListItemClick()` method that shows to the user the selected content updating the adjacent fragment or substituting the list:

```
@Override
public void onListItemClick(ListView l, View v, int position, long
id) {
    if (mIsMultiPaned) {
    //mDetail.updateContent(position);
    } else {
        SmallFragment sf = new SmallFragment();

        FragmentTransaction transaction =
        getActivity().getSupportFragmentManager().
        beginTransaction();
        transaction.replace(R.id.main_container, sf);
        transaction.addToBackStack(null);
        transaction.commit();
    }

    }
}
```

7. Add the definition of the Fragment that will display the details:

```
public static class SmallFragment extends Fragment {
    ...
}
```

8. Implement its `onCreateView()` method, where we simply deflate a layout file representing the contents of the Fragment:

```
public View onCreateView(
    LayoutInflater inflater,
    ViewGroup container,
    Bundle savedInstanceState) {
    View v = inflater.inflate(R.layout.simple, null);

    return v;
}
```

Now it's time to write the layout files.

1. Create a file with the path `res/layout/main.xml`, declaring the single-paned UI:

```
<?xml version="1.0" encoding="utf-8"?>
<LinearLayout xmlns:android="http://schemas.android.com/apk/res/
android"
    android:id="@+id/main_container"
```

```
        android:layout_width="match_parent"
        android:layout_height="match_parent" >
        <FrameLayout
            android:id="@+id/detail_container"
            android:layout_width="0dp"
            android:layout_height="match_parent"
        />
    </LinearLayout>
```

2. Create a file with the path `res/layout-land/main.xml` with the multi-paned UI:

```xml
<?xml version="1.0" encoding="utf-8"?>
<LinearLayout xmlns:android="http://schemas.android.com/apk/res/
android"
    android:orientation="horizontal"
    android:layout_width="match_parent"
    android:layout_height="match_parent" >
    <fragment android:name=
    "org.ktln2.android.packt.FragmentCompatibility
    $SmallListFragment"
        android:id="@+id/list_fragment"
        android:layout_width="match_parent"
        android:layout_height="match_parent"
        android:layout_weight="1"
    />
    <fragment android:name=
    "org.ktln2.android.packt.FragmentCompatibility
    $SmallFragment"
        android:id="@+id/detail_fragment"
        android:layout_width="match_parent"
        android:layout_height="match_parent"
        android:layout_weight="1"
    />
</LinearLayout>
```

## How it works...

The point of the code written in the *How to do it...* section is to create a simple application capable of adapting its content from the context, and of course, make it launchable from any device with a version of Android starting from API level 4.

This is possible using a specific custom class, made available by the compatibility package, named `FragmentActivity`; be aware of this, otherwise the Fragment-related stuff won't work properly.

The code creates a single Activity with two Fragments inside. One is a simple list of random items taken from a simple array and the other is a very simple Fragment containing a constant text. The application chooses how to organize the layout using the device's orientation. When the device is in landscape mode, the Fragments are displayed side by side, otherwise we start with the application showing only the list, and then after selecting one item in the list, we switch to the detail replacing the list with the other Fragment.

It's the job of the Activity class to manage the Fragments displayed. There are two ways to manage the Fragments:

- ▸ **Statically**: By including the Fragment in the XML
- ▸ **Dynamically**: By loading the Fragment during runtime with `FragmentManager`

The important point to note here is that a Fragment defined in the XML can't be removed with `FragmentManager` during runtime, only Fragments loaded dynamically can be removed. This is very important and can result in a very wrong behavior or worse; seems to work correctly, but under the hood it introduces some very nasty bug (for example, pieces of UI that appear multiple times).

 A very useful tool is the Hierarchy Viewer, which is included with the SDK. This tool shows the activities in a graphical hierarchical tree while the application is running. The `.bat` file can be found at `<SDK_ROOT\tools\hierarchyviewer.bat>`.

Let me explain how Android works and how it saves the state of the UI between state transitions.

A state transition happens when an Activity is paused or destroyed, which can happen quite frequently, for example during a phone call (remember, the Android device may be a phone) or even when the device orientation changes!

This last case may be a surprise when your application appears to be working just fine, but then crashes when the orientation changes.

This is because a change in orientation destroys and rebuilds the UI (almost) from scratch. The system makes the `onSaveInstanceState()` method available, which is called before an Activity may be killed and passes to it a `Bundle` instance where we can save all that we think is valuable in order to recreate the actual state. The state can be restored in the `onCreate()` method where the system will pass back the same `Bundle`.

The system saves the state of the UI elements for which an ID has been defined, so for example, if we have an `EditText` method defined into the XML with an associated ID, any text written into it will survive from a state change.

In our code, we have chosen to replace `ListFragment` with the Fragment containing the detail, but in order to do so, we must create it programmatically from the beginning. But here there is a subtle point; since the container view has an ID associated to it, it will have the `ListFragment` saved from the previous state. So we must check if we are coming from a previous state and just in case avoid reattaching the Fragment; the code used is the following:

```
if (savedInstanceState != null) {
    return;
}
```

If instead we are in portrait mode, without previous instances, we can simply attach `ListFragment`, using `FragmentManager` and its methods.

 Note that while with the normal Android's API, `FragmentManager` is returned from `getFragmentManager()` and the Support Library must be called with `getSupportFragmentManager()`.

In order to understand the remaining code, we must master the Fragments' lifecycle, as shown in the following table:

| Fragment | Activity |
|---|---|
| onAttach() | |
| onCreate() | |
| onCreateView() | onCreate() |
| onActivityCreated() | |
| onStart() | onStart() |
| onResume() | onResume() |
| onPause() | onPause() |
| onStop() | onStop() |
| onDestroyView() | |
| onDestroy() | onDestroy() |
| onDetach() | |

An Activity and its Fragments have a tight relationship; what is more important for us now is the creation time, that is, when the Activity's `onCreate()` method is called. As stated previously, the Fragment may be directly placed in the XML layout by using a Fragment tag or dynamically loading the Fragment at runtime. In all the cases, the `onCreateView()` method of the Fragment must return this layout.

Notice that only after the Activity's `onCreate()` method has returned can we rely on proper initialization of the content view hierarchy. At this point, the Fragment's `onActivityCreate()` method is called.

## There's more...

Now let's talk about some other options, or possibly some pieces of general information that are relevant to this task.

## Creating the context adapting interface

When we create the two possible layouts of the Fragments, we choose the landscape and portrait orientation as a switch, but this is not completely the correct approach.

We know well how it is possible to provide various versions of the same resource (layouts, images, and so on) by placing it in a directory whose name is appended with some specific qualifiers that identify the configuration under which the resources must be used (in the previous case, layout-land has been used as the directory's name to indicate as configuration to the device in landscape orientation). The qualifiers can be mixed together, but only in a specific order.

From API level 13 (that is, version 3.2), two new qualifiers are available:

▶ w<N>dp: This qualifier specifies a minimum available screen width in dp units at which the resource should be used—defined by the <N> value. This configuration value will change when the orientation changes between landscape and portrait to match the current actual width.

▶ h<N>dp: This qualifier specifies a minimum available screen height in dp units at which the resource should be used—defined by the <N> value. This configuration value will change when the orientation changes between landscape and portrait to match the current actual height.

With these qualifiers, it is also possible to use the extended layout on devices that have, for example, the screen width on portrait mode large enough to contain it. If we decide that the switch happens at 600 dp of screen width, we can place our extended layout XML file into a directory named `res/layout-w600dp/`.

Another trick useful in cases like these is the use of `<include>` and `<merge>` tags into your layout. In this way, we can create only one specific layout file and reference it from another if we think it must be equal. If we want to use `res/layout-w600dp/main.xml` as our real extended layout, we can reference it from `res/layout-land/main.xml` with the following piece of code:

```
<?xml version="1.0" encoding="utf-8"?>
<merge>
  <include layout="@layout/skeleton_extended"/>
</merge>
```

Here we have renamed it to `skeleton_extended.xml`, the multi-paned layout.

The final words are about managing themes and making them as version-independent as possible. If, for example, we want to use a light theme (the default one is dark) and in particular the `Holo` theme (a particular theme included in all Android OS starting from Honeycomb that is a compatibility requirement for Android devices running Android 4.0 and forward) with devices with an API level equal or greater than 11, we need to declare our custom theme. Create two directories, one with the path `res/values/` and the other named `res/values-v11/`.

In the first, create the `styles.xml` file with the following content:

```
<resources>
    <style
            name="AppTheme"
            parent="android:Theme.Light" />
</resources>
```

In the other instead write the following content:

```
<resources>
    <style
            name="AppTheme"
            parent="android:Theme.Holo.Light" />
</resources>
```

Finally insert the following code line in the `AndroidManifest.xml` file as an attribute of the `<application>` tag:

```
android:theme="@style/AppTheme"
```

It's important to note that these considerations don't help the backward compatibility directly, but they avoid the loss of possibilities offered from new devices.

## Menu

Starting with the Honeycomb version, the way the menu is managed is also different. Because of `ActionBar`, now it's possible to present some menu options on it so that it becomes easily accessible. The ratio to be used in choosing the options to place in the ActionBar should follow the FIT scheme—Frequent, Important, or Typical.

So the method used for building the menu, that is, `OnCreateOptionsMenu()`, is called—when an action bar is present—at Activity start (on pre-Honeycomb devices, this function is activated only by pressing the menu button). For example, we can define a simple menu with two options in it, into a file at the `res/menu/main.xml` path.

```xml
<?xml version="1.0" encoding="utf-8"?>
<menu xmlns:android="http://schemas.android.com/apk/res/android">
    <item android:id="@+id/menu_new"
          android:title="New"
          android:showAsAction="ifRoom"/>
    <item android:id="@+id/help"
          android:title="Help" />
</menu>
```

Since we have indicated the `ifRoom` value in the `showAsAction` attribute, this option will be inserted to the right side of the ActionBar (in case there are more options with the same value set, only those that fit into the action bar will be displayed, the others will be shown normally by the menu button).

In pre-Honeycomb devices without ActionBar, all the options will appear normally with the usual menu buttons.

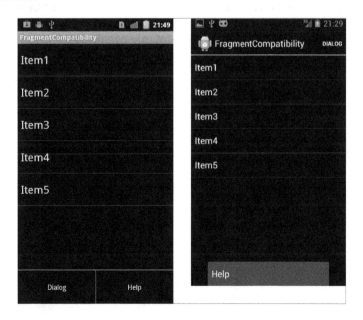

## Fragments without UI

Since the Fragments are components at application level and not at UI level, it's possible to instance these without associating layout elements to them.

We do this programmatically with the add(fragment, tag) function.

This is available with an instance of FragmentTransaction. The tag parameter is a normal string (do not confuse this parameter with the tags used in the View class) that can then be used to find the Fragment with the findFragmentByTag() function.

If you are wondering why you would want to use a Fragment with no UI, keep in mind that in this way Fragments are not destroyed when the UI is recreated (such as during orientation changes).

## minSdkVersion and targetSdkVersion

Since the devil is in the detail, it is important to understand the role of the variables in the <uses-sdk> tag used in AndroidManifest.xml, which expresses the application's compatibility with one or more versions of the Android platform.

As the meaning of minSdkVersion is rather obvious, let me quote an excerpt from the documentation of targetSdkVersion:

> *This attribute informs the system that you have tested against the target version and the system should not enable any compatibility behaviors to maintain your app's forward-compatibility with the target version. The application is still able to run on older versions (down to minSdkVersion).*

> *... if the API level of the platform is higher than the version declared by your app's targetSdkVersion, the system may enable compatibility behaviors to ensure that your app continues to work the way you expect. You can disable such compatibility behaviors by specifying targetSdkVersion to match the API level of the platform on which it's running.*

In our case, we want to create applications installable from devices with API level 4, and in particular, we want to use capabilities introduced with Honeycomb (that is, API level 11), so finally the AndroidManifest.xml file must contain the following content:

```
<uses-sdk
    android:minSdkVersion="4"
    android:targetSdkVersion="11" />
```

For the Eclipse users, it's possible to set these values initially from the Android projects creation wizard:

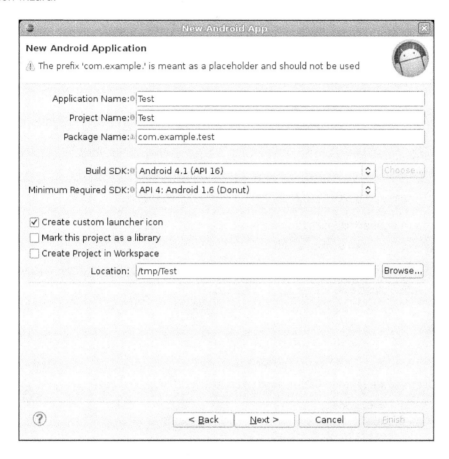

The `targetSdkVersion` is **Build SDK** as set in the shown dialog.

The `maxSdkVersion` must be set manually.

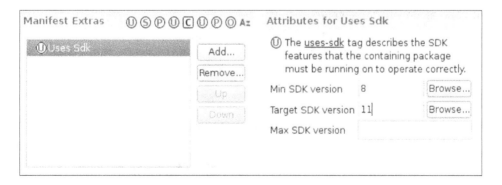

## Dialog

As you can clearly see in the code, there is a special type of Fragment, a `ListFragment`, which is a fragment that displays a list of items by binding them to a data source and exposes event handlers when the user selects an item.

Support Library also provides the backward compatible implementation of the `FragmentDialog` class used to display, obviously, dialog windows. In the documentation, it is explained as follows:

> *A fragment that displays a dialog window, floating on top of its activity's window. This fragment contains a Dialog object, which it displays as appropriate based on the fragment's state. Control of the dialog (deciding when to show, hide, dismiss it) should be done through the API here, not with direct calls on the dialog.*

Let's write some example code in order to show how this is supposed to work:

1. Import ordinary classes that are used to create a Dialog:

   ```java
   import android.app.Dialog;
   import android.app.AlertDialog;
   ```

2. Create a class extending `FragmentDialog`:

   ```java
   static public class DialogCompatibility extends DialogFragment
   {
       ...
   }
   ```

3. Override the method that is used to create the Dialog:

   ```java
   @Override
   public Dialog onCreateDialog(Bundle savedInstan
   ceState) {
   return new AlertDialog.Builder(getActivity())
   .setTitle("Fragment and dialog")
   .create();
   }
   ```

4. Add an option in the menu's resource file:

   ```xml
   <item android:id="@+id/menu_dialog"
           android:title="Dialog"
           android:showAsAction="ifRoom"
           />
   ```

5. Finally, add the following code snippet in the Activity class' `onOptionsItemSelected()` function to call this Dialog:

   ```java
   @Override
   public boolean onOptionsItemSelected(MenuItem item) {
     switch (item.getItemId()) {
   ```

```
        case R.id.menu_dialog:
        DialogCompatibility dc = new DialogCompatibility();
        DialogCompatibility.newInstance()
        .show(getSupportFragmentManager(), "dialog");
        return true;
        default:
        return super.onOptionsItemSelected(item);
    }
}
```

Obviously this is a very simple example and much more could be said, but it's left as an exercise for the reader (as, for example, how to embed a dialog into an Activity).

## VERSION_CODES

Not all the possible problems can be addressed with the Support Library, so it is necessary to learn some ways to manage the different availability of features between versions.

One solution could be the creation of different APKs, one for each particular version of Android, and uploading each one separately on the Android market; this is not particularly smart, since it causes a lot of code duplication and is maintainability hell.

A better solution is to create branches in the interested code, using an `if` statement and checking for `VERSION_CODES`. This is accessible from the `android.os.Build` package and it presents an enumeration of all versions of Android. To be able to check for the actual version at runtime, the `SDK_INT` field must be used in the `android.os.Build.VERSION` package.

At the end, we should write some code similar to the following:

```
if (android.os.Build.VERSION.SDK_INT => android.os.Build.VERSION_
CODES.HONECOMB) {
    // ...
} else if (android.os.Build.VERSION.SDK_INT =>
android.os.Build.VERSION_CODES.GINGERBREAD){
    // ...
}
```

A more sophisticated approach would be to use the resource system in order to set appropriate Boolean variables with values of interest. Suppose we create two `values` files, one with the path `res/values/bools.xml` and with the following content:

```
<?xml version="1.0" encoding="utf-8"?>
<resources>
    <bool name="isHoneycomb">false</bool>
</resources>
```

The other at the path `res/values-v11/bools.xml` with the following content:

```xml
<?xml version="1.0" encoding="utf-8"?>
<resources>
    <bool name="isHoneycomb">true</bool>
</resources>
```

Inside the code, the `isHoneycomb` variable can be referenced with a simple piece of code, as shown as follows:

```java
Resource r = getResources();
boolean isHoneycomb = r.getBoolean(R.bool.isHoneycomb)
```

This can be used directly in the code.

# Loader (Should know)

In this task, we'll show the use of the class called `Loader`, a class specifically intended to do asynchronous work in the background in order to update the application-related data; before the introduction of the `Loader` and related classes, the only way to manage data was using Cursor with some specific Activity class's method:

```java
public void startManagingCursor(Cursor)
public Cursor managedQuery(Uri, String, String, String, String)
```

The problem with this approach is these calls are on the main application thread and can make the application non-responsive and potentially cause the dreaded ANRs!

In the following steps, we will show the code of an application that loads the RSS from Packt's website by an HTTP request to a web server and obviously this can't be instantaneous; here is where the `Loader` class will be used. All of this is done with the Support Library; in this way, the application will be compatible with the previous Android platforms.

## How to do it...

Let's list the steps required for completing the task:

1. First of all, include the necessary Support Library classes:

```java
import android.support.v4.app.FragmentActivity;
import android.support.v4.app.*;
import android.support.v4.content.*;
```

2. Define a class subclassing the `FragmentActivity` class as usual and define the `onCreate()` method that creates the GUI for us:

```
public class LoaderCompatibilityApplication extends
FragmentActivity {
    @Override
    public void onCreate(Bundle savedInstanceState) {
        super.onCreate(savedInstanceState);
        setContentView(R.layout.main);
    }
}
```

3. Define a Fragment that will display the desired data. It's important that it implements `LoaderManager.LoaderCallbacks`:

```
static public class RSSFragment extends ListFragment
    implements LoaderManager.LoaderCallbacks<String[]> {
}
```

4. Implement the adapter for its own data in its `onActivityCreated()`, and more importantly, call Loader by using the `LoaderManager` class' method named `initLoader()`:

```
@Override
public void onActivityCreated(Bundle savedInstance) {
    super.onActivityCreated(savedInstance);

    setListAdapter(
    new ArrayAdapter<String>(
    getActivity(),
    android.R.layout.simple_list_item_1,
    new String[]{}
    )
    );
    /*
    * Differently to what the documentation says,
    * append forceLoad() otherwise the Loader will not be
    called.
    */
    getLoaderManager().initLoader(0, null,
    this).forceLoad();
}
```

5.  Now, it's time to implement the methods defined in the `LoaderManager.` `LoaderCallbacks` interface:

    ```
    public RSSLoader onCreateLoader(int id, Bundle args) {
      return new RSSLoader(getActivity());
    }

    public void onLoaderReset(Loader<String[]> loader) {
    }

    public void onLoadFinished(Loader<String[]> loader,
    String[] data) {
      setListAdapter(
        new ArrayAdapter<String>(
          getActivity(),
          android.R.layout.simple_list_item_1,
          data
        )
      );
    }
    ```

6.  Finally, define the `Loader` subclass (there are two functions, `doGet()` and `getNews()`, that will not be shown here; they simply retrieve the XML and manage to transform it into an array of strings). In particular, implement the `loadInBackground()` method. The reader must note that here we are extending the `AsyncTaskLoader` class that is included in the Support Library:

    ```
    static public class RSSLoader extends AsyncTaskLoader<String[]>
    {
      @Override
      public String[] loadInBackground() {
        String xml = "";
        String[] news;

        try {
          xml = doGet();
          news = getNews(xml);
        } catch (Exception e) {
          news = new String[] {e.getMessage()};
        }

        return news;
      }
    }
    ```

7. Add a simple layout file:

```xml
<?xml version="1.0" encoding="utf-8"?>
<LinearLayout xmlns:android="http://schemas.android.com/apk/res/
android"
    android:orientation="vertical"
    android:layout_width="fill_parent"
    android:layout_height="fill_parent"
    >
    <fragment    android:name="org.ktln2.android.
    packt.LoaderCompatibilityApplication$RSSFragment"
        android:id="@+id/rss_list"
        android:layout_width="fill_parent"
        android:layout_height="fill_parent"
        />
</LinearLayout>
```

## How it works...

The preceding code snippet simply facilitates the synchronization between the Fragment class instance to which the Loader belongs and the Loader itself. The first time the Fragment queries `LoaderManager` by its `initLoader()` method, a new Loader is created using `onCreateLoader()` (if a Loader with the given ID already exists, simply return the old instance without calling this method).

From now on, Loader follows the state of the Fragment (it will be stopped when the Fragment will be stopped) and will call the `onLoadFinished()` method when the data is ready. In the preceding example, the list is updated with the array containing `news` built on `loadInBackground()`.

## There's more...

Now let's talk about some other options, or possibly some pieces of general information that are relevant to this task.

### Low level

Under the hood, an Android application is not a unique block of instructions executed one after the other, but is composed of multiple pipelines of execution. The main concepts here are the process and thread. When an application is started, the operating system creates a process (technically a Linux process) and each component is associated to this process.

Together with the process, a thread of execution named `main` is also created. This is a very important thread because it is in charge of dispatching events to the appropriate user interface elements and receiving events from them. This thread is also called **UI Thread**.

It's important to note that the system does not create a separate thread for each element, but instead uses the same UI thread for all of them. This can be dangerous for the responsiveness of your application, since if you perform an intensive or time expensive operation, this will block the entire UI. All Android developers fight against the **ANR (Application Not Responding)** message that is presented when the UI is not responsive for more than 5 seconds.

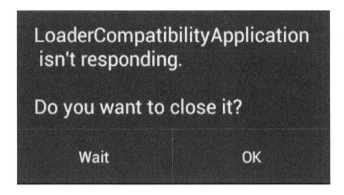

Following Android's documentation, there are only two rules to follow to avoid the ANR:

- Do not block the UI thread
- Do not access the Android UI toolkit from outside the UI thread

These two rules can seem simple, but there are some particulars that have to be clear. First of all, let me show you the simplest way to create a new thread, using the class named `Thread`.

This class implements the `Runnable` interface defined with a single method called `run()`; when an instance of a `Thread` calls its own method `start()`, it launches in the background the instructions defined in the `run()` method. Nothing new for everyone with experience in Java programming; this is plain Java, so it is completely available in all API levels.

For example, if we want to create a simple task that sleeps for 5 seconds, without blocking the UI, we can use the following piece of code:

```
new Thread(new Runnable() {
  public void run() {
    this.sleep(5000);
  }
}).start();
```

All is clear, but in a general case, we would like to interact with the UI, in order to update a progress bar, to show an error, or to change the appearance of a UI element; using an example from Android's documentation, we are tempted to write a piece of code where we update an `ImageView` by using a remote PNG:

```
public void onClick(View v) {

  new Thread(new Runnable() {

    public void run() {

        Bitmap b = loadImageFromNetwork
        ("http://example.com/image.png");

        mImageView.setImageBitmap(b);
      }

    }).start();

}
```

All seems ok, but when running this code, it results in an infamous exception appearing in the application's log:

> *Only the original thread that created a view hierarchy can touch its views.*

This is because `setImageBitmap()` is executed in the thread created by us and not in the UI thread, violating the second rule expressed above (this is not allowed since the UI thread is not thread-safe, that is, it is not assured that concurrent access to an element doesn't cause problems).

Before we solve this problem, let me show you the innermost structures introduced by the Android system to manage threads—the `Looper` and `Handler` classes.

An instance of the first class is simply used to run a message loop in a thread that will be handled by an instance of the second class. On the other hand, a `Handler` instance manages message instances between threads, but its context of execution is the thread where it was initially defined.

In order to understand, it's better to write a complex example involving two threads communicating with messages. Suppose we have a generic Activity class, and inside its `onCreate()` method, we define two threads communicating after every 5 seconds:

```
new Thread(new Runnable() {
  @Override
  public void run() {
    Looper.prepare();

    mFirstHandler = new Handler() {
      @Override
      public void handleMessage(Message message) {
        android.util.Log.i(TAG, (String)message.obj);
      }
    };

    Looper.loop();
  }
}).start();

  new Thread(new Runnable() {
  @Override
  public void run() {
    int cycle = 0;
    while (true) {
      try {
        Thread.sleep(5000);

        Message msg = mFirstHandler.obtainMessage();

        msg.obj = "Hi thread we are at " + cycle;
        mFirstHandler.sendMessage(msg);

        cycle++;
      } catch (java.lang.InterruptedException error) {
        android.util.Log.i(TAG, "error: " + error.getMessage());
      }
    }
  }
}).start();
```

This is how it appears in Eclipse's thread panel when the code is running:

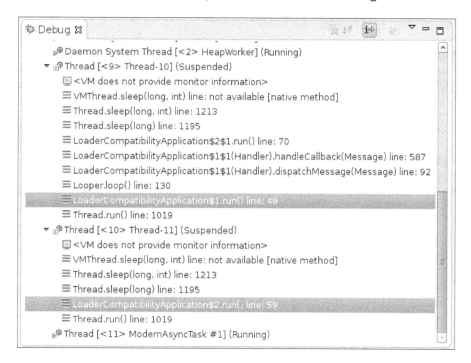

The more fascinating thing is that there is also a possibility to queue the `Runnable` classes to be executed in the original thread of the `Handler` class. Instead of `sendMessage()`, it is possible to use `mFirstHandler.post()` with a `Runnable` class's definition as the argument.

The fundamental point to remember in order to use these classes is to call `Looper.prepare()` and `Looper.loop()` in the `run()` method of the thread and the code related to the `Handler` class in between—that's all.

The only thread that has yet a Looper defined is the UI Thread that makes some methods available in order to post the `Runnable` class instance in it.

Now, back to the earlier problem, let me explain how to solve it using the `Runnable` class; we can post the updating UI code by using a utility method available to any `View`, such as the `View.post(Runnable)` method.

Now, we can substitute the line causing the problem with the following code:

```
mImageView.post(new Runnable() {
    public void run() {
        mImageView.setImageBitmap(bitmap);
    }
});
```

`Looper` and `Handler` are important since they are at the core of the system, and more importantly, they have been available since API level 1, making them good resources for writing the Android applications.

Another important class, available since API level 3, is `AsyncTask`. If you have worked on an application using background threads, it is probable that you have used it since it is intended for this purpose; to facilitate the managing of the threads, and to avoid all the headache and the error-prone code of the `Looper` and `Handler` classes.

Its definition is particular. It uses generics; that is, there are some parameters indicated with `Params`, `Progress`, and `Result` that identify the signature of some functions used internally to manage threads.

In particular, `AsyncTask` has four methods as follows:

- `void onPreExecute()`: Its role is to set up the task.
- `protected Result doInBackground(Params...)`: This is the core of the `AsyncTask` class and your code has to be written here. Just after `onPreExecute()` is terminated, a background thread is created for the execution of this function. It's important to remember not to attempt to update the UI from this function. Use the `onProgressUpdate()` to post updates back to the UI.
- `onProgressUpdate(Progress...)`: This is used to publish progresses in some way.
- `onPostExecute(Result)`: This receives the result of the `doInBackground()` function.

All but the `doInBackground()` function are executed in the UI thread, so it's important to remember not to perform time-consuming work in them.

If we want to replicate the code that downloads a remote PNG and updates an `ImageView` with it, we should write something, as shown in the following code snippet:

```
class PNGUpdate extends AsyncTask<URL, Integer, Long> {
    Bitmap mBitmap;
    ImageView mImageView;

    public PNGUpdate(ImageView iv) {
        mImageView = iv;
    }

    protected Long doInBackground(URL... urls) {
        int count = urls.length;
        for (int i = 0; i < count; i++) {
            mBitmap = loadImageFromNetwork(urls[i]);
```

```
    }

    return 0;
  }

  protected void onPostExecute(Long result) {
    mImageView.setImageBitmap(mBitmap);
  }
}
```

For where we will want to call it, we have to insert a line, such as the following:

```
new PNGUpdate(myImageView).execute(pngURL)
```

What you may have noted is that in the initial steps, when we defined our Loader, we subclassed a class named `AsyncTaskLoader`. It is simply a Loader with an `AsyncTask` inside; the only difference here is that it doesn't get three parameters in its definition, but only one since it's not supposed by a Loader to return information about the status of an operation (for example, no progress bar is shown).

A final note from the documentation about the serial/parallel execution of threads:

> *When first introduced, AsyncTasks were executed serially on a single background thread. Starting with DONUT, this was changed to a pool of threads allowing multiple tasks to operate in parallel. Starting with HONEYCOMB, tasks are executed on a single thread to avoid common application errors caused by parallel execution.*
>
> *If you truly want parallel execution, you can invoke executeOnExecutor(java.util. concurrent.Executor, Object[]) with THREAD_POOL_EXECUTOR.*

## General structure of a Loader

The initial instructions about writing a Loader have used the simple `AsyncTaskLoader` that simplifies a lot for the life of a developer, creating for you the correct subdivision between background threads and UI threads.

This is important, mainly since it avoids wasting your time with little errors, and more importantly, makes the code more modular, avoiding the need of reinventing the wheel. However, now we are to reinvent the wheel in order to understand how to correctly manage the `Loader` classes with your applications.

The Loader is intended to be used with dynamic data, where it is important to be notified for updates in order to refresh the related element of the UI; in order to notify our loader that the underlying data is changed, we'll implement a class named `RSSObservable` that controls that the XML (representing the RSS) is different from the previous version. It's important to note that this is a proof of concept and is not intended to be used in the real world. Both the Loader and the Observable classes download the RSS, causing the drain of the battery (and in some case, you will be billed for the bandwidth).

Once you read this code, try to compare it with the original implementation of the `AsyncTaskLoader` class that you can find in Android's source code in the file `frameworks/base/core/java/android/content/AsyncTaskLoader.java`. Obviously, we are not going to implement all the things that you can find there.

So let's implement our custom Loader:

1. Import the required classes:

   ```
   import android.content.Context;
   import android.support.v4.content.Loader;
   import android.os.AsyncTask;
   import java.util.Observer;
   import java.util.Observable;
   ```

2. Define our custom loader, extending the `Loader` class and indicating the implementation of the `Observer` interface:

   ```
   class RSSLowLevelLoader extends Loader<String[]> implements
   Observer {

       ...

   }
   ```

3. Define the internal variables that will reference the `Task` and `Observable` instances:

   ```
   private Task mTask = null;
   private RSSObservable mTimerObservable = null;
   ```

4. Define the constructor where we initialize all the things needed for the class to work correctly.

   ```
   /*
    * Don't retain a reference to the context in the class since this
    * will / can cause a memory leak.
    */
       public RSSLowLevelLoader(Context context) {
           super(context);

           mTimerObservable = new RSSObservable();
           mTimerObservable.start(mURL);
           mTimerObservable.addObserver(this);
       }
   ```

5. Define a customized `AsyncTask` that returns the data of your choice; in its `doInBackground()` method, simply do the same as the previous example. `onPostExecute()` warns `LoaderManager` of the concluded task.

   ```
   private class Task extends AsyncTask<Void, Void,
   String[]> {
   @Override
   ```

```
    protected String[] doInBackground(Void... params) {
      String xml = "";
      String[] news = null;
      try {
        xml = RemoteHelper.doGet
        ("http://www.packtpub.com/rss.xml");
        news = RemoteHelper.getNews(xml);
      } catch (java.lang.Exception e) {
        news = new String[] {e.getMessage()};
      }

      return news;
    }

    @Override
    protected void onPostExecute(String[] results) {
    // remember: deliverResult() must be called from
    the UI Thread
      RSSLowLevelLoader.this.deliverResult(results);
    }
  }
```

6. Now implement the behavior for the main actions that can be performed on a Loader:

```
@Override
protected void onStartLoading() {
  if (takeContentChanged()) {
    forceLoad();
  }
}
@Override
protected void onStopLoading() {
  if (mTask != null) {
    boolean result = mTask.cancel(false);
    android.util.Log.i(TAG, "onStopLoading() =
    " + result);

    mTask = null;
  }


}
@Override
protected void onForceLoad() {
  android.util.Log.i(TAG, "onForceLoad()");
```

```
    super.onForceLoad();

    onStopLoading();

    mTask = new Task();
    mTask.execute();
}

@Override
protected void onReset() {
    mTimerObservable.stop();
}
```

7. Implement the `deliverResult()` method:

```
@Override
public void deliverResult(String[] data) {
    if (isReset()) {
        // if there is data to be garbage collected do it now
        return;
    }

    super.deliverResult(data);
}
```

8. Write the callback of the `Observer` interface:

```
@Override
public void update(Observable obs, Object data) {
    /*
     * The default implementation checks to see if the
     loader
     * is currently started; if so, it simply calls
     forceLoad().
     */
    onContentChanged();
}
```

9. Write a class representing the `Observable` interface, where we implement the code that watches and notifies us of data changes:

```
public class RSSObservable extends Observable {
    private String mContents = "";
    private String mURL = null;
    private Timer mTimer = null;

    public RSSObservable() {
```

```
      mTimer = new Timer();
    }

    private class InnerTimer extends TimerTask {
      @Override
      public void run() {

        String xml = "";
        try {
          xml = RemoteHelper.doGet(mURL);
        } catch (Exception e) {}
        if (xml != mContents) {
          RSSObservable.this.setChanged();
          RSSObservable.this.notifyObservers(null);

          mContents = xml;
        }
      }
    }

    public void start(String URL) {
      mURL = URL;
      mTimer.schedule(new InnerTimer(), 10000, 20000);
    }

    public void stop() {
        mTimer.cancel();
    }
  }
```

The more cumbersome part is understanding the underlying flow of the Loader. First of all, there are three states in which it can exist. Those are as follows:

▸ STARTED: Loaders execute their loads and notify the Activity class using `onLoadFinished()`.

▸ STOPPED: Loaders continue to monitor for changes, but must not deliver results. This state is induced by calling `stopLoading()` from `LoaderManager` when the related Activity/Fragment class is being stopped.

▸ RESET: Loaders must not monitor changes, deliver results, and so on. The data already collected should be garbage collected.

Each of these states can be reached from the others.

Since all happens asynchronously, it's possible that a notification of data update can reach the `Loader` instance when the state is different from `STARTED`; this explains the various checks present in the code.

One thing introduced in the preceding code snippet, not mentioned in the `AsyncTaskLoader` example, is the Observer/Observable design pattern. The first is defined as an interface and the second as a class, both in the `java.util` package (and both have been available from API level 1, so do not cause compatibility issues). The observer receives notification of updates by the `update()` method, whereas the observable registers some observers (by the `addObserver()` method) to be notified (by the `notifyObservers()` method) when a change occurs.

**A last note**

`cancelLoad()` is not present in the `Loader` class version of the Compatibility Library.

# ActionBar (Should know)

One thing not addressed by the compatibility package is ActionBar, a new UI pattern introduced from Google in the Honeycomb platform. Since this is a very important element for integration with the Android ecosystem, some alternatives are born, the first one from Google itself, as a simple code sample named ActionBar Compatibility that you can find in the `sample/` directory of the Android SDK.

We will follow a different approach, using a famous open source project, `ActionBarSherlock`.

## Getting ready

The code for this library is not available from SDK, so we need to download it from its website (`http://actionbarsherlock.com/`).

You can also download it from the `github` repository of the author; once the archive has been downloaded, you can extract it to a directory of your choice.

## How to do it...

Let's include `ActionBarSherlock` as a library in Eclipse and then create a simple project using it:

1. Open Eclipse and create a new project to import the source files that you can find in the `libraries/` directory of the `ActionBarSherlock` source code. This can be done by selecting **File | New | Other...**.

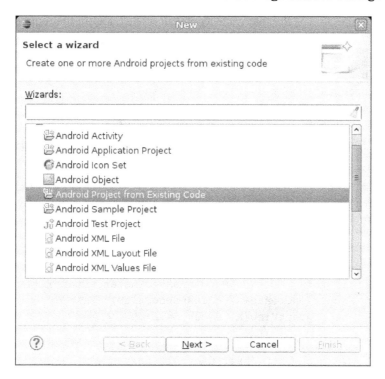

2. Open the project where you want to use the library (otherwise create a new one).

3. Tell Eclipse to use the `ActionBarSherlock` library by selecting the project from the Package explorer and then selecting **Project | Property** from the main menu. A dialog will show up. Now add the library from the **Android** section:

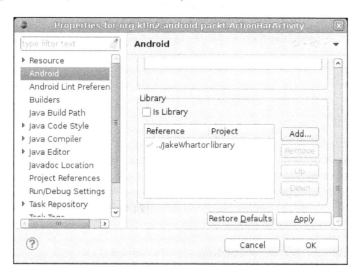

4. In the file containing the main Activity of your project, import the required classes:

```
import com.actionbarsherlock.app.SherlockFragmentActivity;
import com.actionbarsherlock.app.SherlockFragment;
import com.actionbarsherlock.app.ActionBar;
import com.actionbarsherlock.view.Menu;
import com.actionbarsherlock.view.MenuItem;
import com.actionbarsherlock.view.MenuInflater;
```

5. Implement the `Activity` class where the ActionBar will be used, extending `SherlockFragmentActivity`:

```
public class ActionBarActivity extends SherlockFragmentActivity {
    ...
}
```

6. In the `onCreate()` method of the Activity, configure the ActionBar:

```
@Override
public void onCreate(Bundle savedInstanceState) {
    super.onCreate(savedInstanceState);
    setContentView(R.layout.main);

    // if you wan to configure something
    // about ActionBar use this instance
    ActionBar ab = getSupportActionBar();
}
```

7. Add the required the following code snippet in order to create the menu options:

```
@Override
public boolean onCreateOptionsMenu(Menu menu) {
    MenuInflater inflater = getSupportMenuInflater();
    inflater.inflate(R.menu.main, menu);

    return true;
}
```

8. Implement `onOptionsItemSelected()` of the `Activity` class with the desired behavior (here we have shown only a simple toast notification):

```
@Override
public boolean onOptionsItemSelected(MenuItem item) {
    switch (item.getItemId()) {
        default:
            Toast.makeText(this, "Hi!", 1000).show();
    }

    return super.onOptionsItemSelected(item);
}
```

9. Define which menu options you want in the related XML file located at `res/menu/main.xml`:

```xml
<?xml version="1.0" encoding="utf-8"?>
<menu xmlns:android="http://schemas.android.com/apk/res/android">
    <item android:id="@+id/first"
            android:title="First"
            android:showAsAction="ifRoom"/>
    <item android:id="@+id/second"
            android:title="Second"
            android:showAsAction="ifRoom"/>
</menu>
```

## How it works...

Using this external library, we permit our application to have an implementation of the ActionBar UI pattern. `ActionBarSherlock` re-implements most of the core classes that you can find in the normal Android framework. One simple rule to remember is to prepend the word Sherlock to any of the interested classes.

Since it can be tricky remembering which classes belong to this library, let me list these classes:

► `Com.actionbarsherlock.ActionBarSherlock`

► `com.actionbarsherlock.app.ActionBar`

► `com.actionbarsherlock.app.SherlockActivity`

► `com.actionbarsherlock.app.SherlockDialogFragment`

► `com.actionbarsherlock.app.SherlockExpandableListActivity`

► `com.actionbarsherlock.app.SherlockFragment`

► `com.actionbarsherlock.app.SherlockFragmentActivity`

► `com.actionbarsherlock.app.SherlockListActivity`

► `com.actionbarsherlock.app.SherlockListFragment`

► `com.actionbarsherlock.app.SherlockPreferenceActivity`

► `com.actionbarsherlock.view.ActionMode`

► `com.actionbarsherlock.view.ActionProvider`

► `com.actionbarsherlock.view.CollapsibleActionView`

► `com.actionbarsherlock.view.Menu`

► `com.actionbarsherlock.view.MenuInflater`

- ▶ com.actionbarsherlock.view.MenuItem

- ▶ com.actionbarsherlock.view.SubMenu

- ▶ com.actionbarsherlock.view.Window

- ▶ com.actionbarsherlock.widget.ActivityChooserModel

- ▶ com.actionbarsherlock.widget.ActivityChooserView

- ▶ com.actionbarsherlock.widget.ShareActionProvider

If some problem occurs, remember to double-check whether you have used the correct class and not imported the one from the Support Library or the original framework.

This library tries hard to maintain an API compatibility with the original ActionBar. The only difference to remember is to substitute getActionBar() with getSupportActionBar() and to use getSupportMenuInflater() instead of getMenuInflater().

ActionBarSherlock is built on top of the Support Library, so in order to obtain FragmentManager, you must use the getSupportFragmentManager() function.

## There's more...

Now let's talk about some other options, or possibly some pieces of general information that are relevant to this task.

The ActionBar is not only a *bar*, a visual element, but it's also the gate to a bunch of new UI functionalities; in the following sections, we'll show some of these functionalities and how to use it.

### Home button

From the start, the Android platform has made available a **Back** button with which one can step back during the navigation between activity and applications. To allow a more structured navigation, the **Up** button was introduced to permit a user to create a new task from an activity that does not belong to the original task that created it (it's not completely true, since if the original application is the same, no tasks are created).

For example, we start a news reader and then we choose a specific news item that we want to share with our friends by sending it via e-mail; in order to do so, we launch an *Email* application that is started in the same task of the news reader. If the *Email* application has an **Up** button, clicking on it will start a new task with the *home* Activity of the *Email* application.

What we obtain with the **Up** button is a hierarchical navigation inside the active application. Obviously, the **Up** button should not be present in the main Activity because there is no upward navigation there.

In order to enable the **Up** button in our code, simply activate it by using the following code line:

```
actionbarinstance.setDisplayHomeAsUpEnabled(true);
```

We can now write the code that will handle the click on the icon on the left-hand side of the ActionBar. This code is as follows:

```
@Override
public boolean onOptionsItemSelected(MenuItem item) {
  switch (item.getItemId()) {

    case android.R.id.home:

    Intent intent = new Intent(this, MyOwnActivity.class);
    intent.addFlags(Intent.FLAG_ACTIVITY_CLEAR_TOP);
    startActivity(intent);

    return true;

    default:
    return super.onOptionsItemSelected(item);

  }
}
```

Remember only that the **Up** button is represented on the ActionBar with a widget having `android.R.id.home` as an identifier.

## Action view

Another UI pattern from the ActionBar is the **action view**. It is possible to associate a particular widget to an action item. A widget here is, a visual element that can be expanded to occupy all the available space of the ActionBar; in the following code, we will implement a fake search entry—initially on the ActionBar there is only the **Search** button:

After selecting this element, it will appear expanded, as shown in the following screenshot:

1.  Import the required classes:

```
import com.actionbarsherlock.view.MenuItem;
import com.actionbarsherlock.view.MenuInflater;
import android.widget.EditText;
```

2. Implement the method of the `Activity` class used to create the menu:

```
@Override
public boolean onCreateOptionsMenu(Menu menu) {
  MenuInflater inflater = getSupportMenuInflater();
  inflater.inflate(R.menu.main, menu);

  MenuItem menuItem = menu.findItem(R.id.search);
  menuItem.setOnActionExpandListener
  (new MenuItem.OnActionExpandListener() {
    @Override
    public boolean onMenuItemActionCollapse(MenuItem
    item) {
      return true;
    }

    @Override
    public boolean onMenuItemActionExpand(MenuItem item)
    {
      return true;
    }
  });
  EditText fakeSearchView =
  (EditText)menuItem.getActionView();

  return true;
}
```

3. Define the XML file for the menu with an action view:

```
<?xml version="1.0" encoding="utf-8"?>
<menu xmlns:android="http://schemas.android.com/apk/res/android">
  <item android:id="@+id/search"
    android:title="Search"
    android:showAsAction="always|collapseActionView"
     android:actionLayout="@layout/action_view"
    />
</menu>
```

4. Define the layout for the action view into a file placed in `res/layout/action_view.xml`:

```
<?xml version="1.0" encoding="utf-8"?>
<EditText xmlns:android="http://schemas.android.com/apk/res/android"
    android:layout_width="fill_parent"
    android:layout_height="wrap_content"
    android:hint="Search"/>
```

This example mimics the example from the Android documentation where the `SearchView` class is used instead. This class is not available with `ActionBarSherlock`, but is planned to be included (maybe) in future releases.

For further information about this issue, please follow the discussion on the github project page at `https://github.com/JakeWharton/ActionBarSherlock/issues/70`.

## ShareActionProvider

An extension to the concept of action view is the **action provider**—a widget that not only controls its appearance, but also extends its controls. An action provider available with the Android framework is `ShareActionProvider` that allows us to easily share the contents showing a menu with some share target in it.

Since we are interested in maintaining backward compatibility using `ActionBarSherlock`, here are the steps necessary to implement this:

1. Import the required classes:

   ```
   import com.actionbarsherlock.widget.ShareActionProvider;
   import android.content.Intent;
   ```

2. Attach an `Intent` to the action provider:

   ```
   public boolean onCreateOptionsMenu(Menu menu) {
       // remember to use getSupportMenuInflater()
       MenuInflater inflater = getSupportMenuInflater();
       inflater.inflate(R.menu.main, menu);

       ShareActionProvider sap = (ShareActionProvider)menu.
       findItem(R.id.share).getActionProvider();
       // be cautious about the parameter otherwise the
       // menu can be empty
       Intent intent = new Intent(Intent.ACTION_SEND);
       intent.setType("text/plain");
       sap.setShareIntent(intent);

       return true;
   }
   ```

3. Define the XML file:

   ```
   <?xml version="1.0" encoding="utf-8"?>
   <menu xmlns:android=" http://schemas.android.com/apk/res/android">
       <item android:id="@+id/share"
         android:title="Share"
         android:showAsAction="always"
         android:actionProviderClass="com.actionbarsherlock.widget.
   ShareActionProvider" />
   </menu>
   ```

In the following screenshot, you can see how the menu item appears:

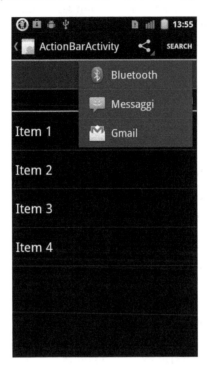

## Contextual ActionBar

The necessity to make simple and quick actions on specific elements such as list items (for example, removing a contact) or copying some selected text into the clipboard, makes the employ of the contextual action bar useful. The appearance of the bar changes so that it can show the specific menu item for the action desired.

Now, let's see how to add a contextual action bar with two action items to your application:

1.  Import all the necessary libraries:

    ```
    import com.actionbarsherlock.app.SherlockFragmentActivity;
    import com.actionbarsherlock.view.ActionMode;
    ```

2.  Implement the `Callback` interface of the `ActionMode` class; it will manage the lifecycle of the contextual menu:

    ```
    private ActionMode.Callback mActionModeCallback = new
    ActionMode.Callback() {

        // Called after startActionMode()
        @Override
    ```

```
public boolean onCreateActionMode
(ActionMode mode, Menu menu) {
// Inflate a menu resource providing context menu
items
MenuInflater inflater = mode.getMenuInflater();
inflater.inflate(R.menu.context_menu, menu);
return true;
}

// Called each time the action mode is shown. Always
called after onCreateActionMode, but
// may be called multiple times if the mode is
invalidated.
@Override
public boolean onPrepareActionMode
(ActionMode mode, Menu menu) {
  return false; // Return false if nothing is done
}

// Called when the user selects a contextual menu item
@Override
public boolean onActionItemClicked
(ActionMode mode, MenuItem item) {
  switch (item.getItemId()) {
    case R.id.action_1:
    mode.finish(); // Action picked, so close the CAB
    return true;
    default:
    return false;
  }
}

// Called when the user exits the action mode
@Override
public void onDestroyActionMode(ActionMode mode) {
  }
};
```

3. Attach a listener to the desired element that will activate the action mode (in this
example, we attach it to the `click` event on a list item):

```
getListView().setOnItemClickListener
(new AdapterView.OnItemClickListener() {
  @Override
  public void onItemClick(AdapterView<?>
  parent, View view, int position, long id) {
```

```
        if (mActionMode != null) {
          return;
        }

        // Start the CAB using the ActionMode.Callback
        defined above
        ActionBarActivity.this.startActionMode
        (mActionModeCallback);
        view.setSelected(true);
        }
      });
```

4.  In an XML file, define the contextual menu layout such as a normal menu:

```
<?xml version="1.0" encoding="utf-8"?>
<menu xmlns:android="http://schemas.android.com/apk/res/android">
    <item android:id="@+id/action_1"
          android:title="Action 1" />
    <item android:id="@+id/action_2"
          android:title="Action 2" />
</menu>
```

The following screenshot shows how the contextual menu will appear:

Remember that the **OK** button (the button at the very left of the bar) simply dismisses the contextual action bar and the system adds it for you.

The obvious extension of this mechanism is the possibility to select multiple elements and to act on it. This exists and it possibly started from Honeycomb, using the `MultiChoiceModeListener` interface that belongs to the `AbsListView` class. The only problem is that it is not available with `ActionBarSherlock`, so as hinted from the original Android documentation, it is better to fall back to a floating contextual menu.

## ViewPagerIndicator

Let's explain how to create a more interesting visual layout for your application, for example, one UI pattern that we see all the time is the "swipey-tabs" one, used in the Android Market.

This UI pattern allows the user to switch between sections of the application, simply swiping left/right and having the title on the tab following the swipe motion (for more technical information about this design, I advise you to read the post from an Android Market designer at `http://www.pushing-pixels.org/2011/08/11/android-tips-and-tricks-swipey-tabs.html`).

In order to do this, we need to download another library from the web page of its project, located at `http://viewpagerindicator.com/`.

The steps required to add this library to our project are the same as those shown at the start of this section. Only keep in mind that the path to the library is where you have extracted it.

Now, we are ready to add `ViewPageIndicator` to your application:

1. Import the correct classes:

```
import com.actionbarsherlock.app.SherlockFragmentActivity;
import com.actionbarsherlock.app.ActionBar;
import android.support.v4.view.ViewPager;
import com.viewpagerindicator.TitlePageIndicator;
```

2. Create an Activity class subclassing `SherlockFragmentActivity` and implementing the `TabListener` interface:

```
public class ActionBarActivity extends SherlockFragmentActivity
implements ActionBar.TabListener {

...

}
```

3. Implement the `onCreate()` method where we set the layout and configure the ActionBar; since we are creating a tab-driven application, we have to set `NAVIGATION_MODE_TABS` as the navigation mode:

```
@Override
public void onCreate(Bundle savedInstanceState) {
   super.onCreate(savedInstanceState);
   setContentView(R.layout.main);

   ActionBar ab = getSupportActionBar();
   ab.setNavigationMode(ActionBar.NAVIGATION_MODE_TABS);

   ViewPager pager =
   (ViewPager)findViewById(R.id.pager);
   pager.setAdapter
   (new TabsAdapter(getSupportFragmentManager()));

   //Bind the title indicator to the adapter
   TitlePageIndicator titleIndicator =
   (TitlePageIndicator)findViewById(R.id.titles);
   titleIndicator.setViewPager(pager);
}
```

4.  Create a subclass of the `FragmentPageAdapter` class that will bind each tab to a specific fragment (here we have used a unique fragment class called `DummyFragment`, not implemented, that simply shows a simple text):

```
public class TabsAdapter extends FragmentPagerAdapter {
  public TabsAdapter(FragmentManager fm) {
    super(fm);
  }

  @Override
  public Fragment getItem(int position) {
    return new DummyFragment();
  }

  @Override
  public int getCount() {
    return 3;
  }

  @Override
  public CharSequence getPageTitle(int position) {
    return "Page " + position;
  }

}
```

5.  Implement the `TabListener` interface in the Activity class that reacts to the events that will happen on tabs:

```
/*
* TabListener interface's methods
*/
public void onTabReselected(ActionBar.Tab tab,
FragmentTransaction ft) {
// User selected the already selected tab. Usually do
nothing.
}

public void onTabUnselected(ActionBar.Tab tab,
FragmentTransaction ft) {
}

public void onTabSelected(ActionBar.Tab tab,
FragmentTransaction ft) {
}
```

6.  Define a layout with `TitlePageIndicator` (double-check that the fully qualified name used as the tag is correctly entered):

```xml
<?xml version="1.0" encoding="utf-8"?>
<LinearLayout xmlns:android="http://schemas.android.com/apk/res/
android"
      android:orientation="vertical"
      android:layout_width="fill_parent"
      android:layout_height="fill_parent"
      >
      <com.viewpagerindicator.TitlePageIndicator
          android:id="@+id/titles"
          android:layout_height="wrap_content"
          android:layout_width="fill_parent" />
  <android.support.v4.view.ViewPager
      android:id="@+id/pager"
      android:layout_width="fill_parent"
      android:layout_height="wrap_content"
      />
</LinearLayout>
```

What we obtain is an application where the various Fragments served from the `ViewPager` class are inserted, one for each tab, and the `TitlePagerIndicator` class furnishes us with a visual effect when the transition between tabs happens. The following screenshot shows how the tab part appears in our application (obviously, it is not possible to show the animation on paper):

**Thank you for buying
Instant Android
Fragmentation
Management How-to**

# About Packt Publishing

Packt, pronounced 'packed', published its first book *"Mastering phpMyAdmin for Effective MySQL Management"* in April 2004 and subsequently continued to specialize in publishing highly focused books on specific technologies and solutions.

Our books and publications share the experiences of your fellow IT professionals in adapting and customizing today's systems, applications, and frameworks. Our solution based books give you the knowledge and power to customize the software and technologies you're using to get the job done. Packt books are more specific and less general than the IT books you have seen in the past. Our unique business model allows us to bring you more focused information, giving you more of what you need to know, and less of what you don't.

Packt is a modern, yet unique publishing company, which focuses on producing quality, cutting-edge books for communities of developers, administrators, and newbies alike. For more information, please visit our website: www.packtpub.com.

# Writing for Packt

We welcome all inquiries from people who are interested in authoring. Book proposals should be sent to author@packtpub.com. If your book idea is still at an early stage and you would like to discuss it first before writing a formal book proposal, contact us; one of our commissioning editors will get in touch with you.

We're not just looking for published authors; if you have strong technical skills but no writing experience, our experienced editors can help you develop a writing career, or simply get some additional reward for your expertise.

## Android 3.0 Application Development Cookbook

ISBN: 978-1-84951-294-7        Paperback: 272 pages

Over 70 recipes covering every aspect of Android development

1. Written for Android 3.0 but also applicable to lower versions

2. Quickly develop applications that take advantage of the very latest mobile technologies, including web apps, sensors, and touch screens

3. Part of Packt's Cookbook series: Discover tips and tricks for varied and imaginative uses of the latest Android features

## Android NDK Beginner's Guide

ISBN: 978-1-84969-152-9        Paperback: 436 pages

Discover the native side of Android and inject the power of C/C++ in your applications

1. Create high performance applications with C/C++ and integrate with Java

2. Exploit advanced Android features such as graphics, sound, input and sensing

3. Port and reuse your own or third-party libraries from the prolific C/C++ ecosystem

Please check **www.PacktPub.com** for information on our titles

## Android Database Programming

ISBN: 978-1-84951-812-3          Paperback: 212 pages

Exploit the power of data-centric and data-driven Android applications with this practical tutorial

1. Master the skills to build data-centric Android applications

2. Go beyond just code by challenging yourself to think about practical use-cases with SQLite and others

3. Focus on flushing out high level design concepts, before drilling down into different code examples

## Android Application Testing Guide

ISBN: 978-1-84951-350-0          Paperback: 332 pages

Build intensively tested and bug free Android applications

1. The first and only book that focuses on testing Android applications

2. Step-by-step approach clearly explaining the most efficient testing methodologies

3. Real world examples with practical test cases that you can reuse

Please check **www.PacktPub.com** for information on our titles